THE MAGPIE'S TALE

NICK BUTTERWORTH & MICK INKPEN

Text and illustrations copyright © 1988 Nick Butterworth and Mick Inkpen
This edition copyright © 2015 Lion Hudson

The right of Nick Butterworth and Mick Inkpen to be identified as the authors and
illustrators of this work has been asserted by them in accordance with the Copyright,
Designs and Patents Act 1988.

This story first published by Candle Books in 2006
in *Animal Tales*. USA edition published
by Zonderkidz ®.

Published by Candle Books
an imprint of
Lion Hudson plc
Wilkinson House, Jordan Hill Road,
Oxford OX2 8DR, England
www.lionhudson.com/candle

ISBN 978 1 78128 173 4

First edition 2015

A catalogue record for this book is available from the British Library

Printed and bound in China, November 2014, LH06

THE MAGPIE'S TALE

JESUS AND ZACCHAEUS

NICK BUTTERWORTH & MICK INKPEN

CANDLE BOOKS

Hello, I'm a magpie. I live in this sycamore tree.

You see the gold ring I'm holding in my beak? I found it. Well, I pinched it really. I used to have lots of stolen things in this nest. Not any more.

Let me tell you the story. It all began yesterday afternoon…

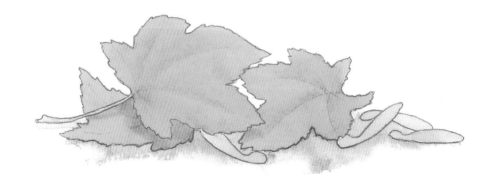

It's a hot day and I'm sitting out of the sun guarding my stolen treasure.

Suddenly I hear the sound of people laughing.

Down below a large crowd is gathering. That's odd. Usually nothing happens around here in the middle of the afternoon.

The people have lined up along the street. They seem to be waiting for someone. I wonder who it is. He must be important.

Look, even Zacchaeus has come out to see. He's the short, fat man who lives in the big house on the corner. Nobody likes him much. He collects the taxes. They say he's a cheat.

Zaccheus is too short to see over the crowd. He's trying to push his way to the front. But he's too fat to squeeze through, and the people won't let him past.

They're pretending not to notice him at all. Nobody likes Zacchaeus.

Now he's coming over to my tree. He's climbing up to get a better view! But his short legs won't reach the branches. He's puffing and panting and going red in the face.

Quickly! The important man will be here soon! Go on Zacchaeus, you can do it!

Just in time Zacchaeus scrambles into the tree. The crowd starts to cheer and everybody presses forward.

'Hooray, here comes Jesus!'

I can just see his face through the leaves. But who is Jesus? He doesn't look important at all. Not like a King, or a General.

By the look of him, he's not even rich. Just an ordinary man.

Jesus walks up to my tree, stops, and looks up through the branches. Perhaps he has spotted my treasure sparkling in the sun.

Does he know I stole it? What does he want?

'Zacchaeus, come down,' says Jesus with a laugh. 'I'd like to stay at your house today.'

Zacchaeus nearly falls off his branch. What a surprise. Why would anyone want to stay with Zacchaeus? Nobody likes Zacchaeus.

Zacchaeus climbs down and Jesus says hello. It's very strange. He speaks to Zacchaeus like an old friend.

The crowd don't like it at all.

'Why choose Zacchaeus? He's a cheat and a thief!' says one woman.

Now Zacchaeus speaks out loud, for everyone to hear.

'I'll give half of everything I own away,' he says, 'and everyone I've cheated I'll pay back four times over.'

The people are amazed. What has happened to Zacchaeus? He's like a different man.

Since then I've taken back everything I stole. The things from my nest have been turning up all over town!

This golden ring is all that's left.
I pinched it from the big house on the corner. Zacchaeus left it on the windowsill.

He'll be pleased to get it back,
I should think.